To Ch...

100Th love

on ther BIRTHDAY

1   The St. Kilda 'Parliament' which required neither police force nor justiciary to regulate life on the group of islands in its care. The main island, Hirta, lies over 100 miles off the west coast of the Scottish mainland

2   (*overleaf*) 'The Iron Duke in Bronze by Steell' – Sir John Steell's famous statue of the Duke of Wellington – forms the foreground of this view of the North Bridge taken about 1885

Victorian and Edwardian

SCOTLAND

from old photographs

Introduction and commentaries by

C. S. MINTO

B. T. BATSFORD LTD

LONDON

B. T. Batsford Limited,
4 Fitzhardinge St, London W1
Printed and bound in Great Britain by
Jarrold & Sons Limited, Norwich, Norfolk
First published in 1970
7134 0114 1

*To my wife who has put up uncomplainingly with
photographic disruptions of her domestic arrangements for
all of the years I most care to remember.*

CONTENTS

ACKNOWLEDGMENTS

So much help has been forthcoming from so many sources that it is difficult to assess to whom most thanks are due but perhaps I may be forgiven for expressing first my gratitude to the staffs in the local history departments of my own library for producing both suitable prints and suggestions for further sources, and especially to Dr. Isabel Frances Grant, now of Edinburgh, founder of Am Fasgadh Highland Folk Museum of Kingussie, for allowing me the run of the magnificent collection of folk life material which she presented to the Edinburgh Public Libraries some years ago. As a starting point this was invaluable. Nos. 76, 109, 150, 157, 158, 162, 174, 183, 185, 188, 189, 195, 200 and 205 are all reproduced from prints in this collection and many other pointers to, for instance, G.W.W. negatives in Aberdeen, were received from it. Next in importance are certainly the Wilson Collections themselves, Aberdeen University having supplied contact prints for nos. 1, 5, 12, 41, 42, 48, 50, 52, 53, 58, 77, 78, 88, 90, 99, 114, 115, 125, 184 and 190, and Aberdeen Public Library's albums and files having yielded nos. 57, 60, 61–67, 83, 85, 87, 91, 97, 110, 149, 151, 154, 156, 167, 181, 186, 187, 192, 203 and 204.

Airdrie Public Library supplied nos. 128, 130, 166, 191 and 197; Clydebank Public Library no. 47; Dumfries County Library nos. 127, 134–136, 141, 142, 168 and 182; Dundee Public Library nos. 68–75 and 101; Hamilton Public Library nos. 137–139 and 159; Kilmarnock Public Library nos. 132 and 133; Kirkcudbright County Library nos. 145–147 and 193; Paisley Museum nos. 129 and 165; The School of Scottish Studies (Edinburgh University) nos. 120, 124, 152, 176 and 196; Shetland County Library nos. 93–96, 161, 164, 199 and 201; Wigtown County Library nos. 143 and 144. Private Individuals loaned a number of prints for copying purposes, those used being nos. 106 Mrs. M. J. M. Irons, now of Clydebank; 155 Mr. Patrick Murray; 160 and 194 Mr. I. R. Grant – both of Edinburgh.

Edinburgh Public Library's files, in addition to those listed as in the Grant Collection, brought to light nos. 3, 4, 6–10, 13–18, 19, 21, 23–32, 34–38, 44, 45, 51, 54, 59, 79, 89, 103, 104, 107, 108, 113, 116, 117, 119, 121, 123, 148, 153, 163, 169–173, 175, 177, 198 and 202.

In addition the Author and Publishers wish to thank the following for illustrations appearing in this book: William Gordon Davis Esq. for no. 82; Messrs. F. Frith and Company Ltd. for nos. 43, 46, 118; Messrs. Judges nos. 20, 22; Radio Times, Hulton Picture Library nos. 39, 40, 49, 81, 84, 86, 102, 105, 111, 112, 122, 140; The Science Museum, London nos. 33, 55, 56, 126, 131; The Trustees of the Victoria and Albert Museum nos. 98, 100 and Messrs. E. R. Yerbury and Son for the Balmain photographs nos. 2, 11, 14, 15, 18. Lastly, illustrations nos. 80 and 178 came from the Publishers' own collection.

To all these sources of material, public and private alike, the author's thanks are due for making what might have been a burdensome undertaking enjoyable and at times exciting. They are most gratefully rendered.

INTRODUCTION

As the sun went down, the scenery became more and more beautiful, the sky crimson, golden-red and blue, and the hills looking purple and lilac, most exquisite, till at length it set, and hues grew softer in the sky and the outline of the hills sharper. I never saw anything so fine.

Queen Victoria: *Leaves from the Journal of Our Life in the Highlands 1848–61*

Some forty years ago a book was published which quickly became recognised as a classic in its field, a most valuable contribution to the understanding and appreciation of Scottish scenery. *The Face of Scotland* by Harry Batsford and Charles Fry has since had many printings with only minor textual emendations and has not to this day been superseded. The authors concerned themselves with the Scottish landscape and the typical buildings which adorned it but not with the people and their jobs. The present book, by contrast, sets out to emphasise the latter though not to the extent of eliminating landscape entirely.

For your author the important words in the title are 'from old photographs' for it is only in this connection that he would claim some special knowledge based on many years of collecting in his official capacity for the files of his library's local history divisions. This said, it should perhaps be added that the practice of photography has been a lifelong pleasure beginning with a plate camera (primitive by today's standards) not that far removed from the apparatus used to produce the photographs in this volume. Many early excursions involved the carrying around of a half-plate camera with its slides and tripod weighing in all some two stones, but that effort was as nothing compared with the transporting problems of the early users of 'view' cameras which were up to six times as bulky and correspondingly heavier. Landscape photography in those days was not a one-man operation and it is not surprising that commercial exploitation of the popular demand for single photographs and albums was in the hands of a number of firms which was small indeed in relation to the proliferation of portrait studios.

The two big names in Scotland were Valentine's of Dundee and Wilson's of Aberdeen, though most districts and all the towns with the possible, and curious, exception of Glasgow, had well-known professional landscape photographers catering for a mainly local market. Though the Valentine firm had been in the view trade for some years before photography became popular in this connection the beginnings of their great photographic enterprise was roughly contemporary with Wilson's in the 60's of last century. As time went on neither firm confined itself to Scotland, Valentine's sending photographic teams to the other counties of the British Isles and Wilson's penetrating the continent of Europe and still further afield. For many years Valentine's maintained files of their photographic negatives but during the course of a recent change of ownership many of these files were unfortunately destroyed before a more enlightened management came to the rescue of what was left. Original Valentine negatives are thus disappointingly few when compared with the massive collection of Wilson negatives, some 25,000, now cared for by the University of Aberdeen and prints in albums presented by the son of the founder of the firm – George Washington Wilson – to the Aberdeen Public Library. The whereabouts of many other Wilson negatives, especially those taken by 'G.W.W.' as photographer to the Queen at Balmoral, is known and many hundreds were, lamentably, stripped of their emulsion and used by an enthusiastic gardener in the building of a large greenhouse. Nevertheless, some forty per cent of the 'G.W.W.' pictures sought were found in the University's files and are reproduced from modern prints.

Nos. 63 and 62 of which no negatives are to be found are of particular interest, the first showing how the production of prints was achieved in quantities to meet popular demand and the second, which it would have been especially interesting to study in respect of its technique, showing an early appreciation of how to prove that the camera *can* lie.

Of all the photographs reproduced, roughly one quarter are from the studios of the G. W. Wilson Company and about one tenth from Valentine's, but in spite of the much greater proportion of Wilson negatives preserved this represents not so much the comparative quantity of output as the comparative amount of work done by each firm in the particular field of present interest, that is, urban landscape and people. The contribution of both firms to recording Scotland is outstanding.

The starting point in the collection of photographs was the publisher's own file of some sixty photographs which was reinforced from a wide variety of sources until it became possible by 'selection' day to choose from over four hundred. The basic qualifications were that every photograph should be clearly of the period from the beginning of photography as evidenced by costume or some other element in the photograph itself and that all should be 'live' in the sense of showing daily life in setting or occupation. Some photographs, however, if weak in either feature, were of such obvious merit as to warrant inclusion and publisher and author were fortunate in arriving at nearly the desired total at the first sorting out.

If the selection of photographs included seems haphazard rather than systematic that is because system can only prevail when the field of choice is both wide and uniform in the coverage of its elements. This is not so with photographs taken over a period of steady if unspectacular improvement in the performance of lenses, shutters and negative materials. It was only after the end of the period under review that the great advances in equipment and emulsions were made and it became possible to photograph under almost any condition of lighting, natural or artificial. The uses of 'flash' – magnesium powder or ribbon – were not, of course, unknown before 1900, but interior shots and especially interiors with action were inevitably few and that is why it has not been possible, as would have been desirable, to illustrate anything approaching a fair cross-section of Scotland's varied industries and trades. No Clyde steel works, no Border woollen mills, not even a distillery or a brewery at work. Much as these omissions are to be regretted, there is some compensation to be gained from the pictures of outdoor pursuits of many kinds and it is hoped that the sampling on offer will be of interest to home Scots, to folk of Scots descent overseas, to historians and sociologists and to that indefinable entity 'the casual reader' who makes the profession of librarianship so enjoyable and rewarding.

Having mentioned librarianship, it would be wrong if there was failure at this point to record the debt that this book – and not only this book by any means – owes to the growth of the local history collection in libraries large and small up and down the country and the 'Acknowledgments' (p. viii) offer evidence enough to the help that such libraries have given willingly and enthusiastically. Though the research worker could get along well enough so far as the printed word is concerned if only a few of our great libraries survived some nuclear holocaust, without the 'non-book' material of local libraries and specialist agencies, the picture that he could paint would be of the 'soot and whitewash' nature that both bedevilled and added strength to early photographs. 'Early' is not easy to define in photographic terms but if one accepts that anything taken in the first twenty years of the art is early then the examples on figures 4, 6, 7, 13, 23, 104, 160, 194 of this book come within that category. The story of how the Scottish landscape artist and illustrator David Octavius Hill was first drawn to photography has been told many times but will stand repeating. Having been commissioned to paint a commemorative canvas of the solemn and unhappy 'Disruption' of the Church of Scotland in 1843, he entered into partnership with Robert Adamson (who had been instructed in photography at St. Andrews by his brother John) in order to obtain likenesses of the many worthy men involved in that religious crisis. Thus came about the most famous collaboration in the annals of photography, but it was destined not to last as Adamson died in 1848 at the early age of 27. They used the 'calotype' or 'Talbotype' process patented in England, but fortunately not in Scotland owing to the separate legal structure, by W. H. Fox Talbot employing paper for both negative and positive. This process in improved form continued into the 'fifties by which time the greater speed of operation and clarity of detail possible by the use of glass as a support for the emulsion of the negative was rendering the paper process obsolescent. Belonging to this period, however, are nos. 4, 6, 7, 13, 23, 104, 160 and 194. The remainder vary in date from 1860 or thereby to about 1910 and their present availability is due to the efforts in the past of many local photographic firms from Shetland to Wigtownshire as well as to the 'big two' already mentioned.

Such names as Annan in Glasgow: Burns, Inglis and Balmain in Edinburgh; Ratter in Lerwick; Milne in Aboyne; McIsaac & Riddle in Oban; Young in Burntisland and Bara in Ayr are among those to whose activities this book seeks to pay tribute.

EDINBURGH

We walked industriously through the streets, street after street, and, in spite of wet and dirt, were exceedingly delighted. The old town, with its irregular houses, stage above stage, seen as we saw it, in the obscurity of a rainy day, hardly resembles the work of men, it is more like a piling up of rocks, and I cannot attempt to describe what we saw so imperfectly, but must say that, high as my expectations had been raised, the city of Edinburgh far surpassed all expectation. Gladly would we have stayed another day.

Dorothy Wordsworth, 16th September 1803

3 The West End of Princes Street shows little change today except for street furniture and traffic islands. The prominent buildings are St. John's Church (Episcopalian) and St. Cuthbert's Parish Church set in the gardens below the Castle. c. 1905

4   The Calton Hill about 1844, from a Daguerreotype. Trinity College Church soon, then, to be demolished to make way for the Waverley Station approach lines lies in the middle foreground

5 Princes Street from the Castle: a popular view unchanged in essentials today although most of Princes Street's old buildings have now succumbed to the march of the multiples

6–7 The Scott Monument. Built to the design of a local architect, George Meikle Kemp, this gothic memorial to Sir Walter Scott created great interest as soon as it began to rise above its foundations in 1841. The two views shown are both by D. O. Hill and Robert Adamson and would have been taken in the winter of 1843–44

8   The Scott Monument completed, looking east along Princes Street towards the Calton Hill c.1865

9   Looking east from the Scott Monument. The flat expanse on the right is the roof of the Waverley Market with the notoriously east windy exit from the Station immediately beyond. c.1888

10   West Princes Street Gardens, c.1885. The 'Old Town' skyline shows, from right to left, the Camera Obscura, the spire of the Highland Church, Tolbooth St. John's, the Free Church Assembly Hall and the headquarters of the Bank of Scotland

11   The East End of Princes Street in 1859

12   (*overleaf*) The Lord High Commissioner's Procession to the General Assembly of the Church of Scotland, 24th May 1883. Lord Aberdeen held this office 1881–1885 and again in 1915. The Wellington equestrian statue (see also No. 2) is prominent in front of the main entrance to H.M. Register House

13 The Castle from the Grassmarket. Photograph dated 17th August 1855. This and No. 23
are two of many photographs of Edinburgh and
Scottish scenes taken by the surgeon, Dr. Thomas
Keith, between 1854 and 1857

14 'Charming Birds'. Cage bird seller in St.
Giles Street opposite the Cathedral, the High
Kirk of Edinburgh, and the Heart of Midlothian.
c.1890

15 'Hokey Pokey'. Ice cream seller in the Royal Mile. c.1895. [Nos. 13–16 and 18–23 depict the 'Royal Mile', Edinburgh's famous thoroughfare from the Castle to Holyroodhouse.]

16 In the Lawnmarket. Corner of the West Bow. c.1870. St. Giles Cathedral can be seen in the middle distance

17   Pavement Artist, Lothian Road. c.1903. Note the elegant baby carriage

18 (*facing page*) 'Cocoa-Nut Tam' who died in 1894 was for many years a familiar, if diminutive, figure at his stance near Halkerston's Wynd. 'Cocky-nit, cocky-nit, a penny the bit' and 'Taste and try before ye buy' were his favourite cries. Photographed in 1888

19 The Canongate, the gait or way of the canons from the town to the Abbey of Holyrood, in 1890. Moray House, on the right, is associated with Charles I, with Cromwell and with the signing of the Treaty of Union of the British parliaments in 1707. The bracketed clock on the left marks the Old Tolbooth (town house and jail) of the former separate Burgh of Canongate

20 John Knox's House built in 1490 and supposedly occupied by the Reformer in the 1560's is the sole remaining example in the Royal Mile of a house with timber built galleries—once a common feature. Photograph c.1906

21 The White Horse Close at the foot of the Canongate, c.1900. Here in the seventeenth century the London coach came and went. The buildings have recently been most carefully restored

22 Bakehouse Close, separating Acheson House, now the Scottish Craft Centre, and Huntly House, one-time town house of the Earls of Gordon, now the principal City Museum

23 A Royal Mile close in the 1850's, typical of many which ran down from the ridge of the Old Town to the Cowgate, or South Back of Canongate as it was called in earlier times

24 The 'New' University [1789] on the South Bridge. c.1890. Spire of the Tron Church in the distance

25 Perhaps the most famous photographic studio in the world. Rock House, Calton Stairs, occupied in 1842–3 by Robert Adamson and David Octavius Hill, recognised masters of photography in the earliest days of the art, and later by Archibald Burns, who took this photograph in 1874, A. A. Inglis and F. C. Inglis; only passing out of use as a studio in 1945

26 Cyclists of the Queen's City of Edinburgh Rifle Volunteer Brigade in George Street in 1884

27 Edwardian Hoarding with a fine sense of balance

28 Fishermen's Houses in New Lane, Newhaven, c.1905

29 Edinburgh's Beach. Donkey ride stance on the sands at Portobello

30 An outing to Cramond at the opposite (west) end of Edinburgh's sea coast from Portobello. c.1900. The picturesque houses on the left and the Inn on the right are still features of this pleasant suburb

31 Portobello Beach. c.1910

32 The Fish Market, Newhaven. c.1900

GLASGOW AND THE CLYDE

Glasgow, the chief city of the kingdom next Edinburgh, delightfully situate in a plain and fruitful country is also a perfectly well-built city, divided into four parts by cross streets of a noble width, the houses of stone, most of them five stories high . . . At a corner just where the four prime streets cross, stands the Tolbuith *of stone, very lofty: over the jail, in the public hall, are lengths of all the monarchs of Great Britain, but ill performed.*

John Loveday: *Dairy*, 1732

33   Glasgow Bridge c.1867. On the far bank to the left is the Broomielaw quay from which the Clyde sailings started at this time

34 Main Street, Gorbals, in 1868. The Gorbals, the once notorious slum area has largely vanished. Multi-storey housing now replaces the old insanitary hovels

35 Shops and houses in the Gallowgate as they were in 1868

36 One of the condemned closes off the Saltmarket, 1868

34–37 At the turn of the century the Glasgow Improvement Trust was much concerned over the deterioration of many properties in the older parts of the town. These four photographs are from the Trust's report, 'The Old Closes and Streets of Glasgow', published in 1900

37 The Saltmarket near Glasgow Cross, 1885. The Clyde was once famous for its salmon and here was where salt was sold for curing the catch

39 George Square and the Municipal Buildings. c.1890. The City Chambers, furnished with real Victorian opulence, were opened by the Queen in 1888

38 Argyle Street, then and now one of the city's main shopping thoroughfares c.1885

40 The Trongate. c.1890. The Steeple on the right is all that remains of Tron St. Mary's Church, 1637. Beyond on the left is another of Glasgow's few ancient landmarks, the Tower and Steeple of the Tolbooth (Glasgow Cross), 1626

41 (*overleaf*) 'Doon the Watter' in the 'nineties. The 'Benmore' leaves the Broomielaw for Kilmun, Dunoon, Rothesay and the Kyles of Bute

42   At the Broomielaw, c.1890. The 'Balmoral' sails for Greenock

43   Princes Pier, Greenock, c.1905. As the Clyde became more and more congested with the growth of its shipyards, many of the sailings started from Greenock, Gourock and other ports further down river

44 At the Tail of the Bank, Greenock, where the Clyde estuary opens out. c.1885

45   Gourock and Gourock Bay. c.1880

46   Custom House Quay, Greenock. c.1905

47 Fitting out basin, John Brown's Clydebank Shipyard. 1904. The ships are: the Cunard triple screw turbine steamer *Carmania*, the cruiser *H.M.S. Antrim* and the Edward VII class battleship *H.M.S. Hindustan*

48 The Clyde Steamer *S.S. Columba* at Rothesay, c.1885

49 West Bay, Dunoon, popular Clyde holiday resort. c.1905

50 Wemyss Bay, terminus of the Glasgow and Wemyss Bay Railway and most popular starting point for the short crossing to Rothesay. c.1890

51   Brodick Pier and Goat Fell, Arran. c.1885

ABERDEEN

We came to Aberdeen on Saturday August 21. On Monday we were invited to the Town Hall, where I had the freedom of the city given me by the Lord Provost. The honour conferred had all the decorations that politeness could add, and, what I am afraid I should not have had to say of any city south of the Tweed, I found no petty officer bowing for a fee. The parchment containing the record of admission is, with the seal appending, fastened to a riband, and worn for one day by the new citizen in his hat.

Samuel Johnson: *Journey to the Western Islands.* 1773

52   Sail still predominating in Aberdeen Harbour. Taken from the tower of the Town House, 1882

53 'Friday Rag Fair', Castle Street, c.1880.
Mercat Cross on right. Tolbooth and Town
House towers beyond

54 Union Street looking east, c.1880.
Town and County Bank and Town House
on left. The Salvation Army Citadel in
middle distance

55 (*facing page*) Union Street from Market Street, c

56   The Town House—erected 1867–71 shortly after completion. The hard-wearing local granite looks almost as clean today

57 William Bain's Rosemount Bus. 1888

58 St. Nicholas Street, c.1890

59   The Gordon Highlanders' Kiltmakers at work in the Barracks, c.1900

60   A Surgical Ward in the old Royal Infirmary, Woolmanhill, c.1889

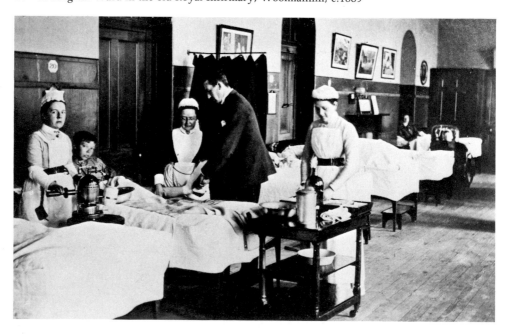

61   Aberdeen Fire Brigade, 1875

62   'Realistic and Surrealistic Photography': an experiment in technique, c.1880. Photograph by G. W. Wilson

63   St. Swithin's Photographic Printing, Finishing and Publishing Works—one of three similar establishments operated by G. W. Wilson in the 'eighties. Activity was seasonal as winter light could well yield as few as a dozen prints from each negative in a day

64 Red Carpet Occasion. Awaiting the arrival of King Edward and the royal party for the opening of the quatercentenary extension of Marischal College, 27th September 1906

65 Union Street at Silver Street decorated for the University Quatercentenary celebrations, 1906

66 The New Market. Opened 1842, burnt out and rebuilt, 1882

67 Market at The Green. c.1905

DUNDEE

. . . a pleasant large populous city, and well deserves the title of Bonny Dundee, so often given it in discourse as well as in song. As it stands well for trade, so it is one of the best trading towns in Scotland, and that as well in foreign business as in manufacturers and home trade. It has but an indifferent harbour but the Tay is a very large, safe and good road, and there is deep water and very good anchorhold almost all over it. Daniel Defoe: *Tour through the Whole Island of Great Britain.* 1724–27

68 A Dundee Tram in the High Street, 1902

69 The Nethergate, looking west, c.1885. Note emigration posters

70 High Street. c.1908

71 The open air Greenmarket, 1898

As I went down the Overgate
  A lassie passed me by
She winked at me wi' the tail o' her eye
  But, mind you, I was fly.

Ricky do dum day, do dum day
  Ricky, dicky do dum day.

                    Popular Song

72   The overgate at Beef Can Close, c.1900

73 Engines on the ill-fated first Tay Bridge in 1878. Hit by gale force winds in a storm in December 1879 the central spans collapsed, carrying a train with 75 passengers into the river

74 The New (and present) Tay Railway Viaduct at the end of 1886

75 Speeding the parting guest. The Royal Visit of Queen Alexandra to Dundee, 1908

THE HIGHLANDS

Yet even the mountains of Glencoe will not leave me with a more vivid recollection than a solitary sea bird, which while we were sitting on a little rocky knoll, dived into the water just below us and when it emerged shook its wings, turned up its white breast, which actually seemed to flash like silver in the light, and sported so beautifully and so happily that I think few sportsmen could have pulled a trigger to destroy so joyous a creature.   Robert Southey: *Journal of a Tour in Scotland in 1819*

76   Ben More and Glen Dochart in the 'seventies. The countryside of the Macnabs

78 Callander Railway Station, c.1875. Callander, known to our television-addicted generation as 'Tannochbrae', is the gateway to the picturesque Trossachs area

Where twines the path in shadow hid
Round many a rocky pyramid.

Scott, The Lady of the Lake

77 Ben Nevis from Corpach, c.1880. The summit is the highest land point in Britain at 4406 feet above sea level

79   The Steamer Pier, Loch Katrine, in the Trossachs, c.1875

80 Grand Chain at a Highland Party, c.1885

81 South Methven Street, Perth, c.1900. Note decorative ironwork

82   The Braemar Highland Gathering in 1909

83   A Stag from the Royal Forest, Glenetive, c.1880

84 The High Street in Crieff, famous for its Hydropathic establishment in Victoria's day. c.1900

85 The Caledonian Canal at Fort Augustus, c.1880. The Canal, through the 'Great Glen' of Scotland, connects the North Sea on the east with the Atlantic in the west

THE ISLES

86 Maclean's Cross, Iona, 1860

Isle of Columba's Cell,
Where Christian piety's soul-cheering spark
(Kindled from Heaven between the light and dark
Of time) shone like the morning star.

Wordsworth

From the lone shieling of the misty island
  Mountains divide us, and a waste of seas
Yet still the blood is strong, the heart is Highland
  And we in dreams behold the Hebrides

The Canadian Boat Song. Author unknown

88 (*facing page*) Getting the Fulmar, St. Kilda. Sea fowl and their eggs, with mutton and milk were the staples of the islanders' diet. They were, by necessity, not great fish eaters as it was only in the most favourable weather that a boat could be launched

87 Mending the Boat, St. Kilda. G. W. Wilson's photographic expedition to the remote St. Kilda took place in 1886 and he brought back a unique record for the time of life on a group of islands that had later [1930] to be evacuated

89 The Palace of Birsay, Orkney, c.1903. The Norsemen knew Birsay as Bergisherad or 'the hunting territory'. The Palace was the home of the Earls of Orkney

90 'The Hoy Express': Ox cart transp
on an Orkney croft. The building beh
was the island's post office. c.1880

91 A South Uist Homestead, 1886. The use of shaped peats as 'cladding' on the walls is an uncommon feature

92 Castlebay, Barra, filled with the boats of the fishing fleet, c.1885

93 Commercial Street, Lerwick, Shetland, c.1890. The flagged streets are still in use today

94 Drying Shetland Shawls after washing, c.1905

95 Steamer Day at Lerwick in the 'eighties

96 Shetland Ponies. The upturned boat used as a shelter or store is still in evidence in the islands

NORTH OF THE FORTH

If there are any public works to be executed, which when completed will prove generally beneficial to the country, it is advisable these works should be undertaken at the present time. This would furnish employment for the industrious and valuable part of the people . . . they would by this means be accustomed to labour, they would acquire some capital and the foundations would be laid for future employments. The Caledonian Canal and roads and bridges are of this description and will not only furnish present employment but promise to accomplish improvements in the future welfare of the country.

Thomas Telford: *First Report, 1803*

97 Pultneytown Harbour, Wick, at the height of the herring fishing season, c.1885

98 Gordon Castle, Fochabers, Morayshire, c.1890

A palace all built with stone, facing the ocean; whose lofty and majestic turrets . . . storm the air and seemingly make dints in the very clouds.

Richard Franck. Seventeenth century

99 High Street, Inverness, c.1880. The Forbes Fountain (foreground) is gone. Faith, Hope and Charity, crowning adornment of the tartan warehouse are gone. The native architecture of the street is almost entirely lost

100 Inverness Castle and Bridge, c.1890. The Bridge is altered, concrete and glass have replaced the houses on the right. Only the Castle remains

101 (*preceding page*) The Fishing and Holiday Resort of Broughty Ferry, near Dundee, c.1909

102 Watching the catch at the Friar's Sholt, Inverness, c.1890

103 In the Fishertown, Cromarty, c.1900. In 1894 nearly 2,300 barrels of herring were cured here

104 Fisherfolk's Cottages, St. Andrews, c.1846. St. Andrews, home of a fine university and of golf, was also a busy fishing port in Victoria's reign

105   College Church, St. Andrews, with the Town Drummer, c.1855

106   High Street, Kinross, in the late 'sixties

107   The Square, Falkland, Fife, c.1900. Falkland Palace (background) was built and used as a hunting lodge by the Stuart kings

108 The Pier at Aberdour, Fife, c.1900. Aberdour, across the Forth, was and is a popular holiday resort with Edinburgh folk. It was also one of the busiest ports of call for the Forth steamer service

109 A Crofter Family, near Ullapool, Wester Ross, c.1880

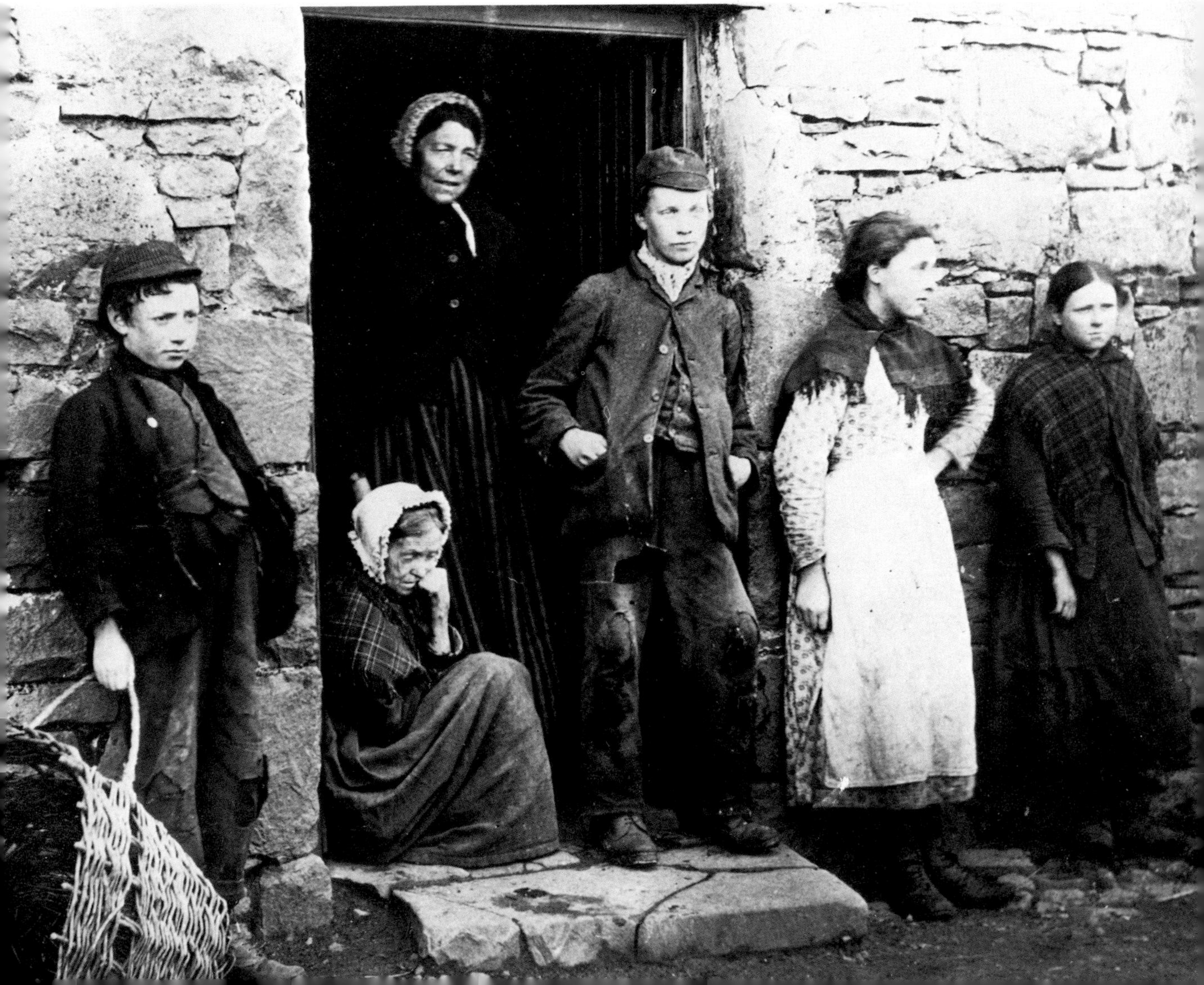

110 A Highland Clachan (small village), Loch Duich, Kintail, Wester Ross. c.1880

111   Oban Bay in Regatta Week, c.1880

112 Crinan Harbour in the 'eighties. The Crinan Canal between Loch Fyne and the Sound of Jura saves a sea voyage of about 130 miles and gives easy coastal access to the Caledonian Canal and the Great Glen

SOUTH OF THE FORTH

. . . the lowlands, consisting of alternate hills and valleys, watered by small but beautiful streams, and cultivated with the utmost care, are interspersed with large and busy towns, attesting everywhere the industry of the inhabitants. From the want of complete surveys, its area has been variously computed; but, calculated from 'Arrowsmith's Map' and as given in the report made to the Board of Agriculture, its extent is 30,238 square miles.

J. H. Dawson: *An abridged statistical history of Scotland.* 1853

113   Fisherwomen on the East Lothian coast, c.1905

114 The Forth Railway Bridge under construction, 1888–89

115 The Forth Railway Bridge completed, 1890. The Bridge is one of the engineering wonders of the nineteenth century and is still as strong and viable today. The Queensferry Passage continued in use at this ancient crossing point until made obsolete by the Road Bridge in 1964

116 High Street, Falkirk, c.1900, with the Town Steeple in the background

117 The Baker's Cart calls at West Pans near Edinburgh, c.1885

118   Fountain Square, Linlithgow, c.1880. There has been a royal palace at Linlithgow since the time of King David I. The ill-fated Mary Queen of Scots was born there in 1542

119   The Railway Company's Bus at Levenhall, near Musselburgh, East Lothian, c.1885

120 Gala Day at Dunbar, E. Lothian. c.1900

121 Haddington, County Town of E. Lothian, c.1900. The tower in the right distance, called 'The Lantern of Lothian', is part of an early Franciscan church

122 North Berwick, East Lothian, famous for its harbour and golf links, c.1895

When stern parental duty's to be done, to be done,
Poor papa's lot is not a happy one, happy one.

123 On the Lothian Coast, c.1885

With apologies to Sir W. S. Gilbert

124 (*preceding page*) Market Square, Melrose, a Border abbey town, c.1900. Note large herd of goats creating considerable interest

125 Abbotsford, Tweedside, home of Sir Walter Scott, from the River. c.1880

126 The Twa Brigs of Ayr, c.1870. Robert Burns in his dialogue poem
'The Brigs of Ayr' makes the Auld Brig say to the New:

> *'Conceited gowk.' puff'd up wi' windy pride'.*
> *This mony a year I've stood the flood and tide;*
> *And though wi' crazy eild I'm sair forfairn,*
> *I'll be a brig when ye're a shapeless cairn.'*

and the prophecy came true in 1877 when the new bridge was swept
away and had to be rebuilt.

127 Dumfries Station, c.1860

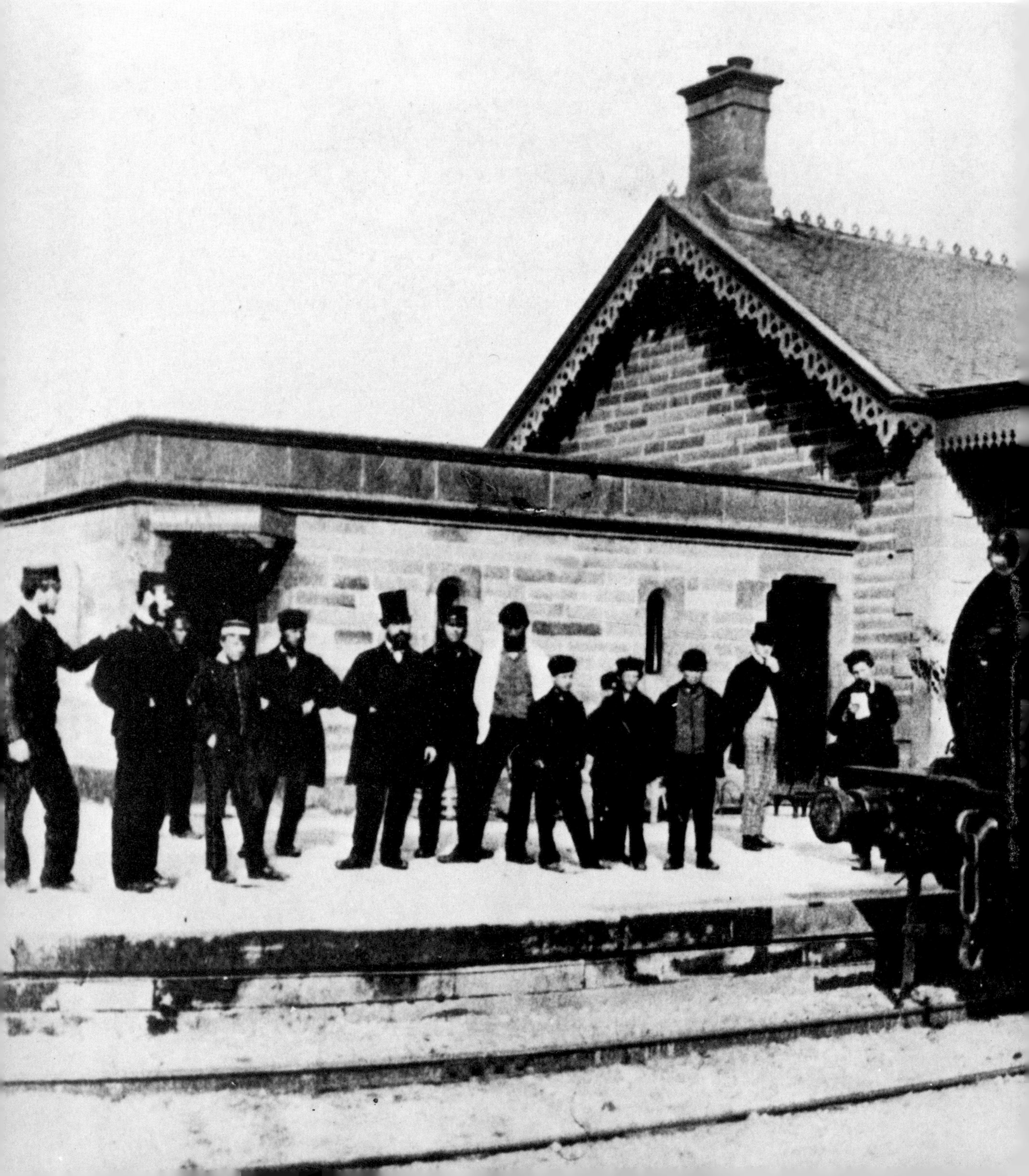

128   Airdrie Cross shortly after the opening of the Airdrie-Coatbridge tram line in 1904

129   Paisley Cross before the demolitions of 1906

130   (*facing page*) The Circus come to town. South Bridge Street, Airdrie c. 1895

131 High Street, Dumfries, c.1870. Ancient and important town, the 'capital' of the south west of Scotland

132 Waterloo Street, Kilmarnock, c.1900. It was in this street that the famous first (Kilmarnock) edition of Burns's poems was printed

133 Interest in 'birds' in a Kilmarnock street, c.1900. The one still able to get away seems intent on doing so!

134 The Glencaple Bus, Dumfries, c.1902. Note lady driver

135 Dancing Bear in a Dumfries street, c.1902

136 Kennedy's Market Garden Stalls below the Mid Steeple, Dumfries, c.1905

137 The School 'Lines' at Hamilton, c.1900. Note the barefoot 'fashion'

138 Black Gold Rush. Digging coal from the bed of the River Avon, near Hamilton, 1880

139 No. 7 Pit, Quarter Collieries, Lanarkshire, c.1905

140   A Visit to Caerlaverock Castle, Dumfriesshire, home of the Maxwells, in 1868

141 A Day in the Park, Moffat, Dumfriesshire, c.1905

142 The Smiddy, formerly the village school, Wamphray, Dumfriesshire, c.1900

143–4 Shipwrecks off the Wigtownshire coast, 1898. The *Firth of Cromarty* (top picture) was out from Glasgow bound for Sydney with some 2,000 *tons* of whisky aboard. Much to the joy of the natives she failed to 'hold her liquor'. Compton Mackenzie recounts a similar incident in his comic novel *Whisky Galore—Tight Little Island* to our American cousins

145 The River Dee at Kirkcudbright frozen in the exceptionally severe winter of 1895

146 One of the Marshall family of the well known Galloway 'Tinkler Gypsies' in camp near Kirkcudbright, c.1910

GALLERY OF FACES

The best way of giving you an idea of the Scotch is to show you in what they principally differ from the English. In the first place (to begin with their physical peculiarities) they are larger in body than the English and the women in my opinion (I say it to my shame) are handsomer than the English women. Their dialect is very agreeable. . . . They are perhaps in some points of view the most remarkable nation in the world; and no country can afford an example of so much order, morality, economy and knowledge amongst the lower classes of society.   Sydney Smith, writing about 1800

147–158 Twelve typical Scots of the period. Most are nameless, but the wise old lady above is Jen Douglas of Kirkcudbright while overleaf is Willie Duff, a kenspeckle figure in and around Dunkeld for many years

149   Stonehaven fisherman

150   Skye crofter fisherman

151   Skye octogenarians

153 'The Shepherdess'

152 Shetland knitter. Note typical high-backed chair

154 *Rosety-Ends*
The Aberdeenshire old village souter (shoemaker)
busy cobbling a ploughman's boot in the sedentary
and contemplative manner of his handicraft

Album caption

155 Falkirk old lady

156 Baiting the Lines, Stonehaven

157 The Laird at ease

158 Carrying home the peats

SOCIAL ACTIVITIES

Now even the poorest labourers take pleasure in the little plots surrounding their homes: the village shops . . . have their windows dressed with engravings of the latest Parisian styles; and the children, barefooted in days of yore, now wear boots and shoes, tacketted and copper toed. In the dead past the only music that ever awakened the echoes of our village was scraped out of the old blind fiddler's instrument of torture, or extracted from that agonising machine—the concertina; but now in all but the poorest houses, you may hear the strumming of little fingers on the keys of a piano.

A. H. Duncan: *Netherton: or, life in a Scottish village.* 1887

159 The Horseless Carriage: Daimler Voiturette, 1897. Six horse power for seven people!

160 'The Presbytery of Dumbarton'. The life of the church was very much the life of the people when this picture was taken to help the artist David Octavius Hill with studies for his pictorial record of the 'Disruption' of 1843

161 Interior of a Shetland crofter's cottage c.1900. Everybody busy, box beds to left and right

162   Wash Day by the Burn

163 Newhaven fishwife on her rounds, c.1900

164 Returning from market, Shetland, c.1907. Note woven paniers

165 Clayholes Fair, Paisley, 1893

166 Ridley motor car, made in Airdrie in 1906 or 7. The Ridley company was one of several small Scottish engineering firms that produced motor cars in the first ten years of this century

167 'Caught on the Hop'.—one of the best known of G. W. Wilson's action photographs

168–9 Coaching days, c.1900. Setting out from Moffat, Dumfriesshire, and [below] in the Pass of Melfort, Argyllshire

170 A boat, a quiet river—what more pleasant memories can childhood hold? The scene is at Cramond Brig near Edinburgh; the date, if it matters, c.1895

171 (*overleaf*) 'Picnic by the Lochside'—the cup that cheers. c.1902

A. Strath.
Jas Anderson.
Bob Kirk.
Jamie Dunn.
D. Park.
Wm Dow
Willie Dunn.
A. Craig
Tom Morris.
Tom Morris Jr
Geo. Morris.

GRAND GOLF TOURNAMENT BY PROFESSIONAL PLAYERS
on Leith Links. 17th May 1867.

172 'Grand Golf Tournament by Professional Players on Leith Links, 17th May 1867'. Though rewards were small the big names in Scottish golf of the day were all there!

173 Curling match at Birnam, Perthshire, between the Birnam and Rohallion clubs. The 'stanes'—from Ailsa Craig quarries off the Ayrshire coast—weighed between 30 and 50 pounds. c.1900

174 Deer stalking in the 'eighties was a serious business—as it still is!

175 The Scottish team (20-a-side in these days) v England in the first Rugby international between the two countries at Raeburn Place, Edinburgh, 28th March 1871. Result: Scotland one goal one try; England, one try

176 Roxburgh Quoiting Club, 1909. Though quoiting did not achieve any general vogue it had staunch adherents in the Borders

177 'Old Firm' clash on neutral ground. Celtic-Rangers game at Cathkin Park, 26th May 1895. Occasion—the final of the Glasgow Cup which Celtic won that season 2–0

179 Group at Haddo House, the seat of the Earl of Aberdeen, September 1884. W. E. Gladstone, with Mrs. Gladstone, visited Lord Aberdeen, prominent Scottish liberal, during the agitation against the House of Lords for rejecting the Franchise Bill

180 Queen Victoria at Balmoral in 1863. With her are John Brown (in kilt) and John Grant, head gamekeeper

181   A solemn party. Sir William Cunliffe Brooke with his wife and guests at Glentanar, Deeside, in 1884. Anyone for tennis?

182   The heyday of the hydro. Moffat Hydropathic Establishment staff. c.1890

OCCUPATIONS

The manufactures of Scotland . . . are of vast extent and employ an immense number of people. The numerous waterfalls—the abundance of coal and iron, so essential for steam power and for smelting and refining the iron ore—our insular position enabling us to obtain supplies of foreign raw materials on the easiest terms—our climate so peculiarly favourable for all sorts of exertion and enterprise—our skill and dexterity in machine making—have all contributed to the high position occupied by Britain as a manufacturing country.

J. H. Dawson: *An abridged statistical history of Scotland.* 1853

183   Fisher girls at Cromarty, c.1905

184 Planting potatoes in Skye. Seaweed was used as fertiliser and the caschrom or foot plough for digging the rows. c.1885

185 Threshing corn with flails in a Shetland barn, c.1890

186 Winnowing and grinding corn in a quern on Skye. c.1885

187 Spinning wool (Skye). c.1885

188 Carding, spinning and winding wool. c.1890

189 'Rooing' or plucking sheep. c.1905

190 Hand loom weaving (Kirriemuir).
c.1880

An' it werna the weavers, what wad we do?
We wadna get claith made o' oor 'oo';
We wadna get a coat either black or blue,
An' it werna for the honourable weavers.

David Shaw, *The Wark o' the weavers*

191 Cotton Mill at Airdrie, 1907

192 The Aberdeen herring fleet puts to sea. c.1885

193 Shoulder net fishing for salmon, River Dee, Kirkcudbrightshire, 1895

194 Fisher girls, Newhaven, c.1845

Wha'll buy caller herrin'?
They're bonnie fish and halesome farin',
Buy my caller herrin'
New drawn frae the Forth.

Lady Nairne

195 (*overleaf*) Herring gutters at Wick, c.1905

196   Fair Isle fishermen, Shetland, c.1908

197 Tobacconist and Newsagent (Airdrie), c.1910

198 The Village shop, c.1880

199 (*facing page*) Crofter casting peats, Shetland, 1909

200 Making a peat carrying basket or 'kashie' (Shetland). c.1890

201 Bringing in the peats in Shetland, 1909

202   William Christie's, the last clay pipe factory in Leith, 1908. The reconstructed workshop can be seen in Huntly House Museum, Edinburgh

203   Granite quarrying at Tillyfourie, Aberdeenshire, c.1890, showing hand and steam boring in progress

204 Hall and Co.'s boatbuilding yard, Aberdeen, c.1870. This firm had a big share in providing for the clipper trade

205   Thatcher at work on a crofter's cottage near Ullapool, Wester Ross, c.1880